From Cotton to Blue Jeans

PROVIDING GOODS

Stephen Thomas

PICTURE CREDITS
Cover: © Getty Images (inset).

page 1 © Richard Hamilton Smith/Corbis; page 4 (bottom left) © Getty Images; page 5 (top) © Richard Hamilton Smith/Corbis; page 7 © Charles & Josette Lenars/Corbis; page 8 (top) © Getty Images; page 9 (top) © Richard Hamilton Smith/Corbis; page 9 (bottom left) © Michael S. Yamashita/Corbis; page 9 (bottom right) courtesy of Renita King/Bradmill Pty Ltd; page 10 (top) © Michael S. Yamashita/Corbis; page 10 © Stock Image Group/SPL; page 11 (top, bottom left, and bottom right) courtesy of Renita King/Bradmill Pty Ltd; page 12 (top) © Roger Ressmeyer/Corbis; page 12 (bottom left) © Lance Nelson/Corbis; page 12 (bottom middle) © Lance Nelson/Corbis; page 12 (bottom right) courtesy of Renita King/Bradmill Pty Ltd; page 13 (left) courtesy of Renita King/Bradmill Pty Ltd; page 13 (middle) © Roger Ressmeyer/Corbis; page 16 (left) © Getty Images; pages 21–23 Robert Chan; pages 24–25 (photos 1–8) Robert Chan; page 25 Robert Chan.

Designed by Kevin Currie.
Prepress by Claire Cole.

Produced through the worldwide resources of the National Geographic Society, John M. Fahey, Jr., President and Chief Executive Officer; Gilbert M. Grosvenor, Chairman of the Board; Nina D. Hoffman, Executive Vice President and President, Books and Education Publishing Group.

PREPARED BY NATIONAL GEOGRAPHIC SCHOOL PUBLISHING
Ericka Markman, Senior Vice President and President, Children's Books and Education Publishing Group; Steve Mico, Vice President and Editorial Director; Marianne Hiland, Executive Editor; Richard Easby, Editorial Manager; Jim Hiscott, Design Manager; Kristin Hanneman, Illustrations Manager; Matt Wascavage, Manager of Publishing Services; Sean Philpotts, Production Manager.

EDITORIAL MANAGEMENT
Morrison BookWorks, LLC

PROGRAM CONSULTANTS
Dr. Shirley V. Dickson, Program Director, Literacy, Education Commission of the States; Margit E. McGuire, Ph.D., Professor of Teacher Education and Social Studies, Seattle University.

National Geographic Theme Sets program developed by Macmillan Science and Education Australia Pty Limited.

Published by the National Geographic Society
1145 17th Street, N.W.
Washington, D.C. 20036-4688

ISBN: 978-0-7922-4718-0
ISBN: 0-7922-4718-3

Product 41958

Printed in China by The Central Printing (Hong Kong) Ltd.
Quarry Bay, Hong Kong
Supplier Code: OCP May 2018
Macmillan Job: 804263
Cengage US PO: 15308030

MEA10_May18_S

Contents

Providing Goods...........................4

From Cotton to Blue Jeans................6

Think About the Key Concepts............17

Visual Literacy
Flow Diagram...........................18

Genre Study
How-to Books...........................20

Denim Craft Book.......................21

Apply the Key Concepts.................27

Research and Write
Create Your Own Directions.............28

Glossary...............................31

Index..................................32

Providing Goods

Think of all the things you use every day. Think of all the food you eat. Think of all the clothes you wear. All the things you eat and use are called goods. Most of the goods you use are made by people. People take things that are found in nature and turn them into goods that other people will want to buy. Jeans, paper, bread, and ice cream are all examples of goods.

 Key Concepts ....

1. Raw materials are gathered, transported, and processed to produce finished goods.

2. The production and distribution of various goods involve different processes.

3. Supply and demand determine which goods are made.

Four Kinds of Goods

Blue Jeans

Blue jeans are made from the cotton plant.

Paper

Paper is made from trees.

In this book you will learn how cotton from plants like these gets made into jeans.

Bread

Bread is made from the grain of the wheat plant.

Ice Cream

Ice cream is made from cows' milk.

From Cotton to Blue Jeans

Do you own a pair of jeans? Most people do. In fact, people in almost every country wear jeans. Men, women, girls, and boys wear jeans. Jeans come in many different colors and styles. What are your jeans like?

Where Do Jeans Come From?

You may wear jeans, but do you know where they come from? Jeans are made from **denim**. Denim is a type of cloth made from a plant called cotton. It takes many steps to change the cotton into jeans.

Many different people wear blue jeans.

Cotton

Cotton is a **raw material**. This means that cotton is found in nature. Raw materials can be made into **goods** that people want. Cotton is found in nature as a plant.

People like wearing cotton because it keeps them cool in summer. In winter, people can wear layers of cotton clothes to keep themselves warm.

raw material
any material found in nature that is used to make products

goods
any products that can be sold

Cotton is a raw material because it occurs in nature.

Growing Cotton

Farmers plant cotton seeds in the spring. The seeds grow into plants with flowers. When the flowers drop off, seed holders, or pods, are left behind. After a while, the pods open to reveal white cotton fibers inside. The cotton can now be picked.

Cotton fibers

Closed cotton pod

Open cotton pod

Seed pods on a cotton plant

The cotton plant grows best in warm places. Look at the map. The pink parts show where cotton grows.

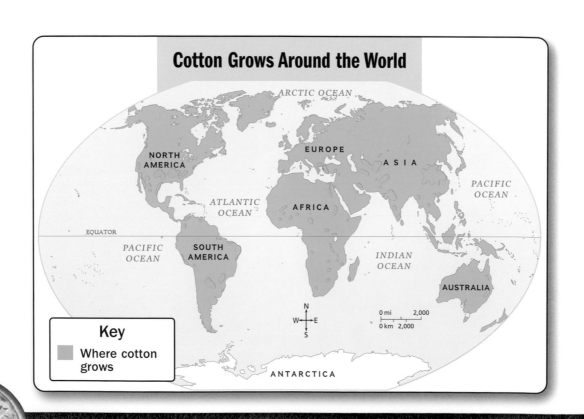

Cotton Grows Around the World

ARCTIC OCEAN

NORTH AMERICA

EUROPE

ASIA

PACIFIC OCEAN

ATLANTIC OCEAN

AFRICA

EQUATOR

PACIFIC OCEAN

SOUTH AMERICA

INDIAN OCEAN

AUSTRALIA

N
W E
S

0 mi   2,000
0 km 2,000

Key
Where cotton grows

ANTARCTICA

Picking Cotton

Most farmers use large machines to pick cotton. The cotton is taken to a **cotton gin**. The cotton gin is a machine that takes the seeds out of the cotton fibers.

The cotton fibers are then made into bales, or large bundles. These bales are **transported**, or sent, to a **mill** to be processed.

Large machines are used to pick cotton.

Cotton gins remove seeds from cotton.

Bales of cotton

At the Mill

At the mill, machines take out any leaves, twigs, and dust from the cotton. The clean cotton is very soft.

Next, a machine twists the fibers into ropes. These ropes of cotton then go through rollers. The rollers stretch out the cotton. Stretching makes the ropes very thin.

Finally, the cotton is spun fast to make it into a cotton thread. Now the thread can be made into cloth.

Twisted ropes of cotton on a machine at a mill

These machines are spinning cotton.

From Cotton to Denim

The cotton is dyed before it is made into denim cloth. Denim is often dyed blue. But some cotton is dyed black or other colors. Cotton can be dyed up to eight times to give it the right color.

The cotton is then woven on a loom to make the denim cloth. The cotton is woven with the threads close together. A lot of threads are used to make the denim thick and strong. The denim is then sent to a factory to be made into jeans.

Dyed ropes of cotton thread

Looms at a denim factory

A worker using a loom

From Denim to Jeans

At the factory, people cut the denim into pieces to make the jeans. They use a special cutting machine. The cut pieces then go to another part of the factory. There, people sew the pieces together on sewing machines.

Jeans are made to be strong. Thick thread is used to sew the jeans so they won't fall apart.

A woman sews jeans in a factory.

The Production and Distribution of Jeans

1. Growing Cotton

Cotton plants are grown. When the seed pods open, the cotton is ready to be picked.

2. Picking Cotton

Machines pick the cotton. A cotton gin then removes the seeds from the fibers.

3. At the Mill

The cotton fibers are cleaned, twisted into ropes, then stretched and spun into thread.

Key Concept 2 The production and distribution of various goods involve different processes.

Getting Goods to Buyers

There are two main stages in getting goods such as jeans to people who buy them. The first stage is the **production** stage. You already read about the production stage for jeans. In the production stage, the cotton goes through the many different processes to make it into jeans.

> **production**
> the processes that turn raw materials into finished goods

The second stage is the **distribution** stage. Distribution is getting the jeans to the places where they will be sold.

> **distribution**
> getting goods to the places where they will be sold

4. From Thread to Denim

The cotton thread is dyed before it is woven into denim cloth.

5. From Denim to Jeans

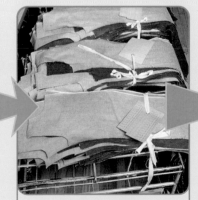

The denim is cut into pieces and sewn into jeans at a factory.

6. Distribution

The jeans are distributed to stores to be sold.

Distributing Jeans

Boxes of jeans are sent from the factory to distribution centers. Distribution centers are places where the jeans are kept before they are sent to stores. Trucks or trains can take the jeans to distribution centers across land. Ships or planes can take jeans to distribution centers overseas.

Stores order jeans from the distribution center nearest them. The distribution center then sends the jeans to the stores on trucks.

Jeans are put onto store shelves so people can buy them.

Selling Jeans

At the clothing stores, the jeans are put onto shelves to be sold. The stores sell different styles and sizes of jeans to suit different people.

Supply and Demand

When a company makes goods like jeans, they look at **supply** and **demand**. Supply is the amount of goods a company makes. Demand is how many goods people want to buy. Companies try to make their supply match the demand.

Demand is affected by **price**. Fewer jeans will sell if the price is too high. Demand can also be affected by fashions and the seasons.

supply
the amount of goods a company makes

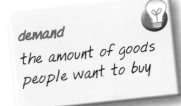

demand
the amount of goods people want to buy

How Supply and Demand Work

If there is more supply than demand, companies will have too many goods that are not sold.

If there is more demand than supply, people won't get the goods they want.

Companies like to make sure that supply and demand are balanced.

15

Fashions

Jeans have been in fashion for many years. But the styles and colors of jeans are always changing. These changes in fashion are called **trends**.

Jeans companies have to follow trends. This way, they can supply people with what they want.

This photo shows boys wearing jeans in the 1950s.

Today's jeans have changed as fashions have changed.

Seasons

The demand for jeans can also change with the seasons. People in hot countries may not want to wear jeans in summer. In winter, there may be more demand for jeans. The jeans companies will need to have a large supply of jeans ready to sell in the winter.

Think About the Key Concepts

Think about what you read. Think about the pictures and diagrams. Use these to answer the questions. Share what you think with others.

1. How are raw materials changed into finished goods? Name the different steps in the process.

2. How do goods make their way to buyers?

3. How do supply and demand affect the production of goods?

4. What are some specific things that suppliers must think about as they produce goods for sale?

Flow Diagram

Diagrams use pictures and words to explain ideas.
You can learn new ideas without having to read a lot
of words.

There are different kinds of diagrams.
This diagram of how goods are distributed is a **flow diagram**.
A flow diagram is pictures and words that show a process.
The diagram shows the order of the different steps in a
process. Look back at the diagram on pages 12–13. It is a
flow diagram of the production and distribution of jeans.

How to Read a Diagram

1. Read the title.
   It tells you what the diagram is about.

2. Read the labels or captions.
   They tell you about the parts of the diagram.

3. Study the pictures.
   Pictures help show the steps. The arrows are pictures,
   too. They show the order of the steps.

4. Think about what you learned.
   Decide what new information you learned from
   the diagram.

How Goods Are Distributed

Factory

Distribution center

Stores

Customers

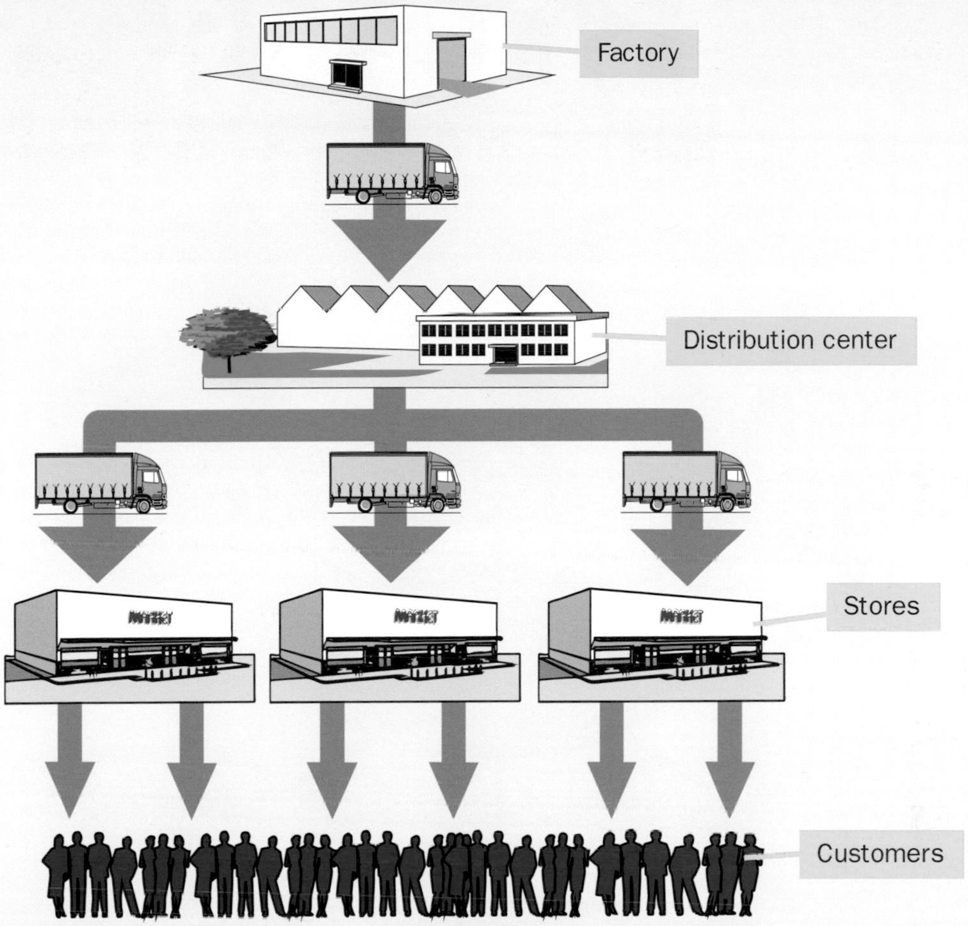

Follow the Arrows

Read the diagram by following the steps on page 18. Write down all the things you found out about how goods are distributed. Explain the process to a classmate. See if your classmate understands the process the same way you did.

How-to Books

The purpose of **how-to books** is to give directions. How-to books take many forms.

You use different how-to books to find out how to do different things. If you want to make things out of denim, you may get some ideas from a **craft book**. A craft book contains **directions** on how to make things.

To use a how-to book, you first find the place in the book that shows you how to make something you are interested in. Then you follow the directions step by step.

Denim Craft Book

This sample shows a set of directions. Directions tell you how to make or do something. These directions are from a craft book about making things from denim.

Iron a Patch onto Denim

The **title** tells what you are going to make.

Old denim can be brightened up with a patch. Follow the steps below to learn how.

The **introduction** gives general information about the craft or task.

What You Need
- Jeans or other denim
- Iron-on cloth
- Permanent markers
- Scissors
- Iron

A **list** of things you will be using

What to Do

Pictures help you understand the instructions.

Instructions tell you step by step what to do.

1. Use the markers to draw a design on the correct side of the iron-on cloth.

2. Cut out your design with the scissors.

3. Have an adult do this step with you. Heat the iron to high. Iron your patch onto the denim.

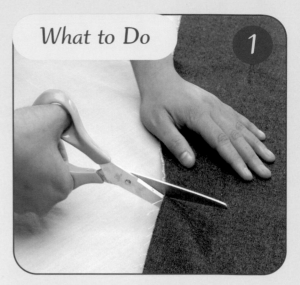

1

1. Cut the denim cloth into two pieces.

Fade-Test Denim Cloth

Have you noticed that each time you wash a pair of jeans they fade a little? This is because the dye in the jeans washes out a little at a time. You can test how denim fades when it is washed. Follow the steps below.

What You Need
- **A new piece of dark denim cloth**
- **Scissors**
- **Bucket**
- **Hot water**
- **Laundry detergent**

4

4. The next day, take the denim cloth out of the water. Squeeze it to remove the water. Rinse the cloth, then hang it up inside to dry.

2. Fill the bucket with the hot water. Mix some laundry detergent into the water.

3. Put one piece of the denim cloth in the soapy water. Leave it in the water overnight.

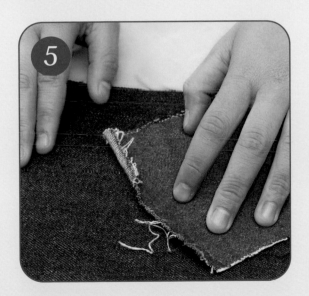

5. Put the washed piece of denim cloth next to the unwashed piece. How much has the washed cloth faded?

6. Cut the washed piece of denim cloth in half. Repeat the steps above with one of the halves. Has the cloth faded some more?

1. Fold the large piece of denim in half on the long side. Make sure the dark side of the cloth is on the inside. You will now have a 15-inch (38-centimeter) square of cloth.

Make a Denim Tote Bag

Denim tote bags are very useful. The denim makes the bags strong. Tote bags can be used for carrying heavy loads like books or groceries. Follow the steps below to make your own denim tote bag.

4. On the top side, use the zigzag stitch to sew each open edge of the cloth. These edges will become the opening for the bag.

What You Need
- 1 piece of denim, 15 inches (38 centimeters) by 30 inches (76 centimeters)
- 2 pieces of denim, each 20 inches (51 centimeters) by 2.5 inches (6.3 centimeters)
- Thread
- Sewing machine
- Ruler
- Iron

7. Fold the two strips of denim in half on the long side, with the dark side of the cloth facing out. Zigzag stitch the edges and the ends of the cloth together.

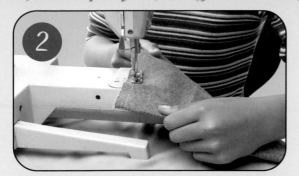

2. Sew a seam along both sides of the folded cloth, but not the top. Sew the seam ⅝ inch (1.6 centimeters) from the edge.

3. Use a zigzag stitch to sew the raw edges of the side seams. The zigzag stitch will stop the raw edges from coming apart.

5. Fold each top edge over so there is a 1-inch (2.5-centimeter) hem. Stitch the hem into place.

6. Turn the bag right side out. With the help of an adult, iron the bag flat.

8. Sew each end of one of the strips of denim on the inside of the bag, 3 inches (7.6 centimeters) from the seams. Repeat with the other strip on the other side of the bag.

Dye Some Jeans

Did you know you could dye your jeans a different color? Your jeans might have faded. Or you might want them to be a different color. Follow the steps below to learn how to dye your jeans. Dyeing can be messy, so ask an adult if you are allowed to dye the jeans before you begin.

What You Need
- **Jeans**
- **Rubber gloves**
- **1 packet of washing machine dye**
- **1¾ cups of salt**
- **Washing machine**
- **Laundry detergent**

What to Do

1. Wash the jeans that you want to dye.

2. Put on the rubber gloves. Keep them on until you have finished dyeing the jeans.

3. Put the dye into the drum of the washing machine.

4. Cover the dye with the salt. Put the damp jeans into the washing machine.

5. Turn the washing machine on using the warm cycle.

6. When the cycle has finished, add some laundry detergent. Turn the washing machine on again. This time, use a hot wash cycle.

7. Hang your jeans out to dry.

Apply the **Key Concepts**

Key Concept 1 Raw materials are gathered, transported, and processed to produce finished goods.

Activity

Choose one kind of goods. Do research to find out what the product is made from. Draw a flow diagram to show the steps in making the product. Be sure to include:
• how the raw material is gathered
• how it is moved to a factory or mill
• how the product is made

Peanut Butter
raw peanuts

Key Concept 2 The production and distribution of various goods involve different processes.

Activity

Continue your research to find out how your product is distributed. Use pictures and captions to show your findings.

truck

Key Concept 3 Supply and demand determine which goods are made.

Activity

Write down any factors that would affect the supply and demand of your product. Ask yourself questions such as:
• what sorts of trends might affect the supply and demand of your product?
• if the price of buying the product went up, what would happen to the demand?

Supply and Demand
_____
_____

Create Your Own Directions

You have read the directions telling you what you can do with cotton. Now it's time for you to think about other things that you can make with cotton. You can write your own directions, then give them to a friend to follow.

1. Study the Model

Look back at page 21. Look at the way the directions are arranged on the page. Read the labels to find the important features of directions. See if you can find the same features on pages 22–26.

2. Choose Your Topic

Now think about other things that you can do with cotton. You may need to do some research. Look at books in the arts and crafts section of the library, or try the Internet, to help you with your ideas.

Directions

◆ The title should tell the readers what they will make.

◆ Include a list of things the readers will need.

◆ Use numbered instructions that are easy to understand.

◆ Use pictures to help explain the instructions.

Cotton Pencil Case

What You Need

- cotton fabric
- thread
- sewing machine

What to Do

1. Fold the fabric in half.
2. Sew the short sides together.
3.

3. Research Your Topic

Think about how you will make what you have chosen. Make notes of the materials you think you will need. Make notes of what you will do.

4. Trial Run

Now get the materials and follow your directions. Change your notes, if you need to, to make your directions clearer.

5. Write the Directions

When you have finished, write down the directions. Use the directions on page 21 as a model. Read over your work. Check your spelling and punctuation.

Follow Each Other's Directions

Now you can share your directions. Follow the steps below.

How to Share Your Work

1. **Trade directions with a friend.**
   Give your directions to your friend. Take your friend's directions to follow.
2. **Read your friend's directions.**
   Think about what materials you will need to follow the directions.
3. **Find the materials you will need.**
   You might be able to find some of the materials at school. You might be able to find some of the materials at home.
4. **Follow your friend's directions.**
   Follow the directions step by step. Use the pictures to help you understand the directions.
5. **Give your friend feedback on the directions.**
   Were the directions easy to follow? Are there ways your friend can make the directions clearer?
6. **Bind all the class directions together in a book.**
   As a group, make a cover for the book. Then bind all the pages together with staples or yarn.

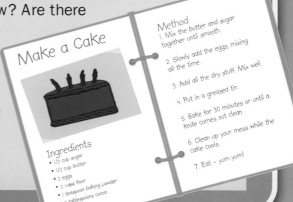

Make a Cake

Ingredients
- 1/2 cup sugar
- 1/2 cup butter
- 2 eggs
- 2 cups flour
- 1 teaspoon baking powder
- 2 tablespoons cocoa

2

Method
1. Mix the butter and sugar together until smooth.
2. Slowly add the eggs, mixing all the time.
3. Add all the dry stuff. Mix well.
4. Put in a greased tin.
5. Bake for 30 minutes or until a knife comes out clean.
6. Clean up your mess while the cake cools.
7. Eat – yum yum!

3

Glossary

cotton gin – a machine that separates seeds from cotton fibers

demand – the amount of goods people want to buy

denim – a strong, thick cloth made from cotton

distribution – getting goods to the places where they will be sold

goods – any products that can be sold

mill – a place where raw materials are processed

price – the cost of a product

production – the processes that turn raw materials into finished goods

raw material – any material found in nature that is used to make products

supply – the amount of goods a company makes

transported – moved from one place to another

trends – changes in the kinds of products people want to buy

Index

company 15–16

cotton 4–13

cotton gin 9, 12

denim 6, 11–13

distribution 13–14

factory 11–14

fibers 8–10, 12

goods 4, 7, 13, 15

jeans 4–6, 11–16

mill 9–10, 12

production 13

stores 13–14